THE SPACE OF JOY

ALSO BY JOHN FULLER

Fiction

Flying to Nowhere
The Adventures of Speedfall
Tell It Me Again
The Burning Boys
Look Twice
The Worm and the Star
A Skin Diary
The Memoirs of Laetitia Horsepole
Flawed Angel

Poetry

Fairground Music
The Tree that Walked
Cannibals and Missionaries
Epistles to Several Persons
The Mountain in the Sea
Lies and Secrets
The Illusionists
Waiting for the Music
The Beautiful Inventions
Selected Poems 1954 to 1982
Partingtime Hall (with James Fenton)
The Grey Among the Green
The Mechanical Body
Stones and Fires
Collected Poems
Now and for a Time
Ghosts

Criticism

The Sonnet
W. H. Auden: a Commentary

For Children

Herod Do Your Worst
Squeaking Crust
The Spider Monkey Uncle King
The Last Bid
The Extraordinary Wool
Mill and Other Stories
Come Aboard and Sail Away

Edited

The Chatto Book of Love Poetry
The Dramatic Works of John Gay
The Oxford Book of Sonnets
W. H. Auden: Poems Selected by John Fuller

THE SPACE OF JOY

John Fuller

Chatto & Windus
LONDON

Published by Chatto & Windus 2006

2 4 6 8 10 9 7 5 3 1

Copyright © John Fuller 2006

John Fuller has asserted his right under the Copyright, Designs
and Patents Act 1988 to be identified as the author of this work

First published in Great Britain in 2006 by
Chatto & Windus
Random House, 20 Vauxhall Bridge Road,
London SW1V 2SA

www.randomhouse.co.uk

Addresses for companies within The Random House Group Limited can be found at:
www.randomhouse.co.uk/offices.htm

The Random House Group Limited Reg. No. 954009

A CIP catalogue record for this book
is available from the British Library

ISBN 0701181109

EAN 9780701181109

The Random House Group Limited makes every effort to ensure that the papers used
in its books are made from trees that have been legally sourced from well-managed and
credibly certified forests. Our paper procurement policy can be found at:
www.randomhouse.co.uk/paper.htm

Typeset by Palimpsest Book Production Ltd, Grangemouth, Stirlingshire

Printed and bound in Great Britain by Mackays of Chatham, plc

CONTENTS

I

THE SOLITARY LIFE

THE SOLITARY LIFE

1 *The Thought*

The hammock takes my length (and half again
For those fanned strings which lift me to their hooks
Sunk in the ash trees) – nine feet perhaps, or ten,
A cradle with a cushion and some books
Slung in the space between two brotherly trees
Whose roots beneath are surely interlaced
Just as their branches are, twin canopies
In paused career, obsequiously placed,
The rooted footmen of my swaying chaise
That hastens nowhere all the afternoon,
Shrugging great arms as if they stood perplexed
At the mind's cross-roads in a sudden blaze
Of sun breaking through leaves, and all too soon
Uncertain which direction to take next.

2 *The Birth*

To be the lazy lord of this long day
Is to have abdicated from much else
And joined the mob of midges at their play,
Hearing the story that the water tells
Beneath their weightless dancing on the stream,
Its variations on the groundbass whose
Continual presence is the sacred theme
That Seneca discovered at Vaucluse:
'Now and for ever, this is what I bring,
Now and for ever, seeping from the earth,
Now and for ever, though I change my course
And muddle meadows, this is what I sing,
A blessing on the moment of my birth,
A wonder at the mystery of the source.'

3 *The Makers*

My head is rocking in the breeze that stirs
The smallest drooping branches of the trees.
My head is full of shadowy characters
In whom I ponder similarities
Of restlessness and longing and a quest
For peace, bewilderment at troubles of
The heart, a contrary desire for rest
From action and a sanctuary from love.
That most are makers is no accident,
For what they made commemorates the mood
Of troubled sacrifice that occupied
Their fertile minds, the endless passion spent,
The endless melancholy that ensued
And haunted their regrets until they died.

4 *The Regrets*

I think of Petrarch at his lonely farm
Beside the rising of a sacred river,
Believing that an Avignon madame
Was cause enough for love to last for ever.
I think of Wagner's Sachs, to whom the *Geist*
Of song, its long tradition and survival,
Was something fine for which he sacrificed
All hope of love, and gave it to his rival;
I think of Pope beside the sparkling Thames,
His bed as empty as his heart was full;
Impetuous Coleridge, that guilty youth;
And Arnold's self-deceiving theorems
That proved a mutual trust impossible,
The solitary life a form of truth.

4

5 The River

For him the wounds of Thun were healed at Dover
When love defied the sundering of the sea.
Yeats, counting swans, discovered one left over
That symbolised his heart's instinctive plea.
The Channel's futile din, the darkening flood,
The churning fountain of a restless heart,
The gorgeous river, stately as the blood
That measured out its rhythms in their art,
All flow within their natural banks, along
The random line geology decided:
The brook in spring echoed the lover's breath,
Midsummer meadows greeted his winning song
And theatres of tragic knowledge guided
Him safely through the estuary of death.

6 The Valley

From the blind valley like a theatre
In green and gilt, rising in tiers of stone
On either side, sheer, semicircular,
You see the compass of the sky, its own
Stage for cloud-performances, a ceiling
For painted tree-tops where a god adores
A lifted nymph and birds perform with feeling
Above the river's chatter and applause.
Below, one aisle's a river, one a field
And one a village in its narrow place
With its extended cart-track wandering through,
And in the bosom of the cirque, concealed
Among gestating rocks, deep at the base
Of the boulder-cliff, a matching disc of blue.

7 The Course

This is the *vallis clausa*, the Vaucluse,
Where waters rise and the world ends for you,
The place where there is nothing left to choose,
The place where there is nothing left to do
But live within the life you have created.
The waters rise because they must. You know
Their winding passage to the sea is fated.
You know the distance that you have to go.
Some trace that devious path time and again
Like pilgrims in the season of their wending
Towards the home to which their spirits ran
As soon as they had wind of it; but then
There are the others for whom thoughts of ending
Can only lead them back where they began.

8 The Source

Bottomless pool, mysterious, still thing!
That seems all surface in its silent home,
Half-stage, half-cave, and rounded like a ring,
Green as the copper of an ancient dome
That skies have stained with weeping, like a shrine
We come to stand around but may not enter,
A glass of some inestimable wine
We may not drink, a maze that has no centre.
Bottomless pool, but turbulent in spring
When the deep waters rise through hidden courses,
Hosing their conduits, flooding their mossy tanks
And bursting to the surface where they fling
Rocks down the valley and the river forces
Its foaming shoulders all along its banks.

9 *The Story*

One day I took my fiddle to Vaucluse
To make the lasses dance. I fell asleep
In the long hot day beside the river whose
Proprietary nymph rose from the deep,
As beautiful as water, took my hand
And led me down between the parted walls
Of its stilled depths to a far wonderland
Of diamonds like solid waterfalls.
She plucked the first, from which a fountain spurted,
And then another six, until the clear
Level filled and slowly rose to stroke
The root of an old fig-tree which (she asserted)
Drank of those waters only once a year!
And then she disappeared. And I awoke.

10 *The Meeting*

Suddenly her face was there before me
And all my self-possession fell away.
The street was silenced when she turned and saw me.
I did not know if I should go or stay.
I might have been that village fiddler dozing,
A fool with fairies. Or a stumbling stranger
Welcomed by fiery angels, not supposing
The sight of them posed any sort of danger.
Her eyes drank mine until my senses spun.
They were like fruit upon a living branch
Torn from the tree of heaven, the leaves her hair,
And I was changed, as night is by the sun.
My brain was Ætna, knees an avalanche.
And still I went on standing there.

11 *The Speaking*

Unshaped, uncoloured and undisciplined,
Trespasser of boundaries, marauder
Of surfaces, the bullying pirate wind
Tugged at my heart in its sublime disorder,
Surged in my throat and issued at my lips.
But just as I was charged for declaration,
It suddenly blew again, the way it strips
A tree of its impulsive foliation.
Just as it takes clouds into custody
And sends them strolling, lifting, lofting, streaking,
Just as it blows the dust and scraps and birds
About, along, away and endlessly.
Resentful witness of my witless speaking,
The wind made off with my expended words.

12 *The Sparrows*

I crawled here, studded with love's deep arrows,
Deep as the blood was slight, and no one knew
I was my story, and the mocking sparrows,
Rehearsing it, confirmed that it was true:
'Ah, Signor Pet-pet-petrarch, is it you?
The quee-quee-queerest of the summer guests,
You look to *us* to see what you should do?
Forgive us, but we must be building nests.'
I am respected here, beneath my trees,
The wounds of life dressed in the salve of art,
The shattered frame propped on a sunny bench,
Where there is consolation in a cheese
And to the silence of an Italian heart
The vulgar sparrows chirp their perfect French.

They guessed the single riddle of the owl
Who gripped the branch and waited for an answer.
They mocked the stateliness of waterfowl
Who wore their their ruffled feathers like a dancer.
There was no colour in their difference,
No pause or circumspection of display,
In their approach no kind of deference,
In their rejection nothing like dismay.
Queen of our nature, how can you explain
The lesson of the sparrows? You proceed
As if your ceremonies licensed their
Effusive cries and your imperious reign
Declared them busy servants of your need
To be obeyed and worshipped everywhere.

14 *The Poet*

And now I play the patient hunter who
Simply by blinking knows the whereabouts
Of all the persons of his retinue
And welcomes them with hideous mild shouts,
Sails like a figurehead upon the flood,
One feathered brilliance from brow to bib,
White as this page on which the sepia blood
Streams like pure logic from the beak-like nib,
Medusa of the dusk, whose hullabaloo
Gathers the living to her frozen page,
Making eternity of our brief minute,
Pale as the moonlight that revealed us to
That beautiful, inconsequential rage,
The heart still beating with her talons in it.

15 *The Ascent*

The impact was complete, of a consummate
Beauty from which one could not look away,
As at a mountain from whose breathless summit
The world itself would lie there on display:
The heights of other mountains, the slow flood
Of seas, the silvery course of rivers, stations
Of trade and discourse, the broad ocean's thud
Against the settled earth, the constellations.
Men climb up there and they admire all this
(My brother puffing up Ventoux and choosing
The harder path – just like his whole career!).
But is the truth found in creation, bliss
In a face, &c? We should be using
Awareness of ourselves instead, that's clear.

16 *The Echoes*

Not mountains, valleys. And not stones but streams.
The quarried profiles pose against the sky,
Sharpened at sunset into apophthegms
That shape the echoes we are answered by.
And I have stared at them too long until
Their beauty turns me to a granite block
Emptied of admiration, emptied of will,
Yielding to them as to a state of shock.
But water answers to our looser shape,
Restores our sense of the large wastefulness
And playfulness of all material things,
Slipping away towards its great escape
Into the indiscriminate, to bless
With silence our insistent questionings.

17 *The Wren*

In and out, in and out of the wall
That borders on the stream, and out and in,
Out and in, busy for spiders all
The afternoon, the truly feminine,
The troglodytic-troglodytic wren
Twitching her stuck tail like a rabbit's scut,
Looking from side to side, wary of men
Like me, and scuttling, tiny as a nut.
Life surges in each negligible vein
To feed her young and keep from harm, no time
For compliments from courtly hearts, the air
Trembling with danger. Still, I feel again
That breeze which rings the changes in my rhyme,
Stirring the laurels, and her golden hair.

18 *The Puzzles*

These are the seasons of the soul: the peace
That comes from contemplation, and the needs
Of human energy; the lovely cease
Of striving, and the wind among the reeds
That blows the lover's usual hunting call,
A flourish from their pipes; the reckless violence
Borrowed from the gods in chasing all
Beauty, and philosophy's shrewd silence.
These moods are much more closely intertwined
Than we suspect, for knowing what it's at
Is body's latest novelty: without
That knowledge were no puzzles that the mind
Could give the body back to solve, and that
The body is too blind to puzzle out.

19 *The Shriving*

Hail to the vignerons of Vacqueyras!
We drank at tables dappled by the sun
And then rode up the hill to Gigondas
Where they were pleased to tap an ancient tun
And talk in slighting terms of Vacqueyras
Where they in turn had criticised their rival:
When Vacqueyras debates with Gigondas,
Claims of the orthodox ensure survival.
It's only when the skies are overcast
That the grape's heretics are seen to yield,
And not until the wine is in the glass
And levelling the future and the past
Is the soul shriven. Now and in the field
The race is Vacqueyras and Gigondas.

20 *The Absence*

Philosophy will tell you life goes on
In all the ways that you expect it to
In China, Rome, and yes, in Avignon,
A place where there is nothing more to do
Than all the things that men and women do.
And so they do them too in Avignon.
In China and in Rome they do them, too.
And so it is that life itself goes on.
Her dreams are not of me, whoever she tells.
Her secret thoughts from me need no concealing.
She lies, but not to keep the truth from me.
Where she keeps house, she keeps it for someone else.
No one, I least of all, knows what she's feeling
And if she must confess, it's not to me.

21 The Philosopher

You are a manuscript upon the shelf,
More readily, perhaps, upon my knee!
My advocate and teacher, better self,
The friend and guardian of morality.
Classic in Africa, you are one half
Of all I think, Carthage your Avignon
Where they still venerate the Golden Calf,
Bishop, philosopher and saint in one.
And there's the rub, for what are manuscripts
Weighed dram for dram against eternal life?
And where is Virgil in the scale with Christ?
Ruins of Rome are like the bones in crypts,
And politics an ever-sharpened knife.
We wait in vain to be emparadised.

22 The Debate

I see the bishop standing by my bed
In the deliberate way that bishops do
When they are keen to talk, and also dead.
I know that he will stay the whole night through
And talk past many candles in a play
Of moving shadows till unnoticed dawn
Lightens the skylight and I greet the day
With the long cogitation of a yawn.
'How may we dare to hope to have no hope?'
(Long answers here.) 'Was man created sordid
Or were those parts acquired through sin, and when?'
'Where can we find the veritable Pope?'
(A shrug.) 'Is virtue better unrewarded?'
'How may we know our innocence again?'

23 *The Occupation*

Ah, innocence! that has no consciousness
Of how the future judges us, and may
Be totally transfixed by things of less
Importance than a perfect summer day.
It is not innocence itself you need
But knowledge of the truth: that nothing lasts.
Hope is a prisoner of the future. Freed,
It is awareness, and it is the past's.
For sixteen years you have put up with an
Invasion of the homeland of your heart,
Laura your Hannibal, the prisoner's rope,
The future's hostage, and no single man
To force the insistent general to depart
But you, and some vain sacrifice of hope.

24 *The Summer*

The branches of the trees are low with leaves.
Each dawn I hear the sound of some newcomer
Describing light in thrilling recitatives.
I call each flower to the school of summer
And learn anew their rank and friendship as
They skip down lanes and tumble through the hedges.
And I'm in love once more with what the season has
To sing of green stuff leaking from its edges.
Abundance of this sort compels the mind
To its old quarrel with futurity:
One year the summer will be here, not I.
We think ourselves unique among our kind.
The day will shine on other shapes, not me.
The birds that sing will sing and never die.

25 The Harvest

Smiles from the marketmen of Malaucène
Who stirred the glistening olives in the press.
I smiled at them. They smiled at me again,
Smiles from the well of a profound tristesse.
They stirred their crop and crushed its weight between
The heavy rollers of my heart. I tore
Each sorrow from its dusty branch, the green
That's almost grey, the green that I foreswore,
And gave them harvest. And the oil like ink
Redeemed those sorrows, as the lifted wine
Seals with its glow the memory of shame.
Summer like grief will tell us what we think,
Distil our life to something almost fine,
The slow gathering of a well-known name.

26 The Death

Well, there is death in nature after all
And we are not in heaven (shall we be?),
Nothing to please us, everything to appal.
The worst of death is its uncertainty.
Imagine the Olympian secretariat
If, like Ovid, I made them countersign
An eminently sane requirement that
Her death be 'late, and only after mine'!
Her death came first, and now I must believe
In unexpected answers to such prayers.
For in a dream she came to me and said:
'I am in heaven, so you must not grieve.
God knows he is the wisest of delayers,
Since I am living now, and you still dead.'

27 The Glory

Words, words, words. I planted them
Like bays, for fame not immortality.
The sixth of April was my Bethlehem.
The sixth of April was my Calvary.
Temporal glory, not the eternal life,
Moved in my verses like the sound of water.
I chose a muse above an earthly wife.
I gave the world a book but not a daughter.
Words taught the scholar how to play a role,
A knight in love, a soldier in the wars,
Or anything I wished to be, to fashion
Signs of my presence, mirrors of the soul
That shows your own in mine, and mine in yours,
And recreate both beauty and its passion.

28 The Process

'Sacred because unfathomably deep.'
So Seneca. To live within that sound,
Nursing old tears hidden too well to weep,
Is certainly to dwell on hallowed ground
Where what escapes the spring does so with glee
Over the trout-pools and rock-crowded falls
And passes to the mill's machinery
Where paddles beat out rags in dripping stalls.
The formes of pulp are lifted and couched well
On felt, until a hundred are so laid,
The water pressed away. I write a sonnet
Whose logic underlines this parallel:
Out of old clothes is shining paper made.
Out of old lives are poems written on it.

29 *The Relics*

And after all, paper is all we know
And yet we feel antiquity about us.
The world's a room in which we come and go
And once the world was much the same without us.
A field turns up the blades of victory
Although it is forgotten now who won.
That fig-tree is the grandson of the fig-tree
That was the great-great-grandson of the one
That Petrarch knew, and now in Luberon
You can go strolling up a brambly plateau
And see Lacoste, the home of the de Sades
(Laura's relations, it is said), all gone
When revolutionaries sacked the chateau
And sold its stones for middle-class façades.

30 *The Portrait*

And where now is that sacred image sent
By his friend Martini, as if he meant to say:
'Here, I believe you! She's magnificent!
This paint is what she is, and will be, day
After day, escaping age, safely within
The frame I gilded so it matched her hair
Already gold, framing the brow and chin,
"*Capei d'oro a l'aura sparsi*", where
The breeze that loosened it was her as well,
All pagan nature in the favourite pun
That came to serve you as a kind of motto.'
Where is Martini's portrait? Who can tell?
When Petrarch died, there were no Lauras, none,
Only a fine Madonna by Giotto.

31 *The Truth*

Newman's idea of the stream of truth:
Not pure at source, but after it's been tested
By meeting its terrain; not in its youth
But in its deepening bed and long-contested
Banks, where controversy strengthens its
Resolve, and in its fall and gravity
It steers its course between plain opposites
And so proceeds in fullness to the sea.
Is this, then, Petrarch's faith in what the human
Spirit seeks? What love is all about?
Something at first not obvious at Vaucluse,
Something about the sacredness of woman,
Something of birth and water, something devout,
Some long-concealed, impossible good news?

32 *The Reconciliation*

Her life, unknown, has been redeemed for us
Not by the monstrous feelings of the poet
(Which, don't we feel, are something like a fuss
Since even he seemed happy not to know it)
But by our sense of what the likelihood
Might be. And everything that in her case
Gave her a chance to choose what kind of good
Lies in a certain life in a certain place
Must be worth more than all the lines he wrote.
Augustine would have said so. The true hope
Of man in woman is longing reconciled
With its alternative, the asymptote
Of deference in his short-sighted scope,
The woman's choice, the mother and the child.

33 The Meditation

Still as I am, it is the nearby stream
That carries me. The mind slides over stones
In little disconnected moods that seem
Like water as it imitates the tones
Of confidential speech: interminable
Narrative about some past event,
Inconsequential, self-important babble
That lulls an anaesthesia of assent.
The stream is speaking of its origin
A field or two above, that much is clear.
That always was its subject, is so still,
And will be till at last the sun goes in
And there is no one left alive to hear
It take its idle gossip down the hill.

34 The Future

As from the highest hills the heather's sprue
Pales to the purplish distance of the sea
And the effusive stream enlarges to
The silver windings of the estuary,
So we are certain that the future brings
A largeness with that vagueness and a kind
Of sublimation of the little things
That constitute the hunger of the mind.
Then, we assure ourselves, our purposes
Will be fulfilled and all dissatisfactions
Resolved into a settled state of being
When the last irritating error is
Discovered, every detail of our actions,
Like a long calculation, now agreeing.

All that we worship is an absolute
You'd maybe call the world behaving well.
Its core is tenderness: the poise of fruit,
Its bloom and moisture as it starts to swell;
The baby sleeping at the trickling breast
And sucking now and then as it recalls
Why it is tucked in there; we know the best
We wish for lies within our own four walls,
The welcome shape of things as what they are
And our entirely willing doing of them.
We say their beauty pleases us, but clearly
They are our life's realised phenomena.
Our recognition is the way we love them
For being hints of our perfection, really.

2

COLERIDGE IN STOWEY

COLERIDGE IN STOWEY

'Why we two made to be a Joy to each other, should for so many
years constitute each other's melancholy – O! but the melancholy is
Joy –'
                                                              S. T. Coleridge

Wrestling the challenge of Infinity
To Personality, I sometime heard
The Bride's voice, distant, from her bower,
Less often now. I argue with my self;
Certain, therefore, of half a certainty
Before the mists assert their mistiness
And leave me without a Way.
                              And now at eve,
Where once beneath a sprawling tent
Of dappled leaves and aromatic keys and flowers
I set my creaking chair's unequal feet
Upon the bulging roots that sank down deep
Into green Somerset for sustenance,
It has become my wintry pleasure here
To find my self not in an obscure wood,
But somehow lost beneath a single tree
That like a cage lowers its naked branches
Towards the icy bareness of the soil.

Truly a prison that the season locks
As a mind is locked by thoughts that put it there!
Unfeeling, inward cogitations, blind
To the light that still streams from a chilly West.
The satisfaction of the solitary
Is to think to be defined by others' thoughts
Concerning him, enjoying their concern,
Relishing misery so long as he
Is made its object, like a Pietà.
The heron has the patience to be patient,
Though there be never a fish in sight.

Would he may not starve! And furthermore
It were unnecessary that the worm
Make friends; and therefore to its social sense
The convivial temper is unknown. I hail
These stoic fellow-creatures in my soul!
Heron, worm and poet share the doom
Of labouring for a scant reward!
                                        Inside,
The coals burn thinly on their wretched altar.
The Shadow Folk on walls and ceilings, guardians
Of our quieter Selves that after kettle-quarrels
Settle to nodding by a flickering stove,
Make mocking Panoramas of such battle.
They are our little household gods, masters
Of a moment that undoes all painful knots,
Loosening shapes to fly like smoke and light
And makes our stillness move still, though still, in fancy.
For there is joy upon the cess of words
Spoken in heat, joy in admonishment,
Joy in the melancholy pilgrimage
Our staffs pace out in almost unison
Greater than joy itself.
                                        And here is Hartley,
Little dear Heart, patient philosopher,
His palms clasped to his lips as if to mock
Some grave proposal, not of his usual play
But of a Voyage back to his beginning,
A novel understanding of his place
In the unfixed perplexing scheme of things.
I offer him a piece of cheese, entire
For the moment that its crumbliness allows,
And gladly he takes it as one who reconciles,
In gracious condescension, the Many with
The One.
                        Our very first posterity
Is but a small parcel of infinite Joy
Troubled only by the animal spirits

Which went into its making, and our wonder
At the hysteroplast is but a glimpse,
A memory of our own origins,
Grieving with a full heart that such fresh Joy
Will soon become a Melancholia
Like ours.
                The woman gives him a bowl of soup
As though he were not mine and certainly
Not hers, but as though my many faults had left him
The better deserving of such charity.
I am to her merely a child, as he is,
Our occupations equal as separate play
In the one chamber.
                   His cheese falls in the soup,
And I talk with the Shadow Folk to tell them
The Mountains of the Moon are like the veins
In cheese, or embers of a fire, that make
Faces of our present disposition
Out of old satisfactions. And I think
Of him in his first slumbering stillness where
Feeding with ruddy cheek against the moon's
Blue vein-of-a-mountain, the new god's
Baby feet twitched in clouds of linen.

Enthusiastic in his saintliness,
The bridegroom ordered harps, which rendered praise
To him for his forgetting lamps, and now
All that I say is what I know is true,
Though with a bitter voice that may be challenged
As the unspeakable, irrelevant
To ears that have no need to hear it, and thus
One with the freezing blast that rises now,
Rattling the branches of its cage. O most
Miserable! O vain shadow of shadows!
I have seen the depth of shame, the bride weeping.
I have, outrageously, spoke my own sentence,
And our triangulation, like the new maps

Commissioned by the Ordnance for the War,
Creates a blankness in the living world
That may not be traversed.
                                        All evening
I sit in the parlour in my great-coat like
Satan hiding wings . . .

3

ARNOLD IN THUN

ARNOLD IN THUN

Up and down with their bells,
Bells in each hand: such a din,
Bells on the thigh and the knee.
Some were as big as a hive,
Great bells fit for a cow
Leading her white herd across
The lesser slopes of an alp,
Others the size of a head,
Judith with Holofernes'
Dripping with gory tones,
And some only tiny, untimely
Ripped from the necks of calves,
Harsh notwithstanding, a dead
Sound like the chink of a spoon
Cast in the empty soup-bowl.

Unenchanting display!
What was it for, he wondered?
What was it that brought him here
To the dullest place on earth?
Something had lured him here,
Not the brass chatter of bells
But a renewal of vows
Made at affinity's shrine
Long since, and duly pondered.
Lured by an old lure, then,
Holy enough in intention,
Lured by the instance that proved
Thrillingly true an idea
Long-suspected to be
Faulty in some sort (though
Often put to the test).

Lured by one case that upheld
Frequently-questioned laws
Worth the upholding since men
Swore to them in their hope
(Still swear, insanely, in hope)
That if a contract be made
Soul to soul it should stand
Sanded and signed and sealed,
Permanent in God's eyes,
Binding its parties for life.

Lured by a pair of blue eyes
Lit at the fuse of a smile,
Turning as if by chance
To the far side of the room
Where in a stupor he stood.
Lured by a knotted scarf
Pulled apart at that knot,
Hair shaken loose, the dress
Paisley in pattern,
Salmon and ultramarine
Commas nestled together,
Sweet in their cotton mosaic,
Spawning their swelling shapes,
Little suggestive tails,
Seeds and floating leaves
That in a moment bestowed
Buoyancy on her, a lift
Upwards to life, a rich
Swimming in nature's signs.

So he was lured, and again
Drawn to this red-tiled town
Stuck in its neck of lake
Like a worm-eaten bung
Stopping the flood of a jar,
Halting the River Aare

For only a moment with piers,
Walls and sluices and falls,
The navigation of trade.
Lake-side town, antique,
Finding itself somewhere
Between the city of bears
And the barely passable Alps,
Town of uncertain trade,
Timber and corn and fish,
Cheese, too, from uplands where
Once together they walked,
Laced at the elbow and wrist,
Smiling out at the view,
The feminine peace of the lake.

Lures of all kinds that draw
Men across half of Europe
Drew him to the Hotel
Bellevue's enormous divan,
Circular meeting-place,
Studded upholstery
Like a train waiting-room,
Every seat facing outwards,
Leaves about a stem
Idly plucked off in turn,
Assignations fulfilled,
Casual glances complete,
Taking it all in at once.
Hither and thither the trays,
Laughter over the fetched
Luggage, travellers' tales.
There he was handed the square
Message on silver, inert
Till secretly read and conned,
So much casual ink
Looped and twirled on the paper
Looking as if a fly

Staggered in tipsy joy.
Eyes take a glance round the room,
Certain that they're unobserved
Since all the guests have their own
Secrets, kept to themselves,
Not to be shared or told.

So, was he loved? Or was
Love only traffic of vague
Psychological states?
Such are the ways of hotels,
Places of casual tryst,
Places of endless waiting,
That in the course of things
Nothing much comes to light,
Nothing is done, nothing said.
Families come and go,
Opportunists at large
Make their obsequious bows,
Businessmen entertain,
Bargains struck about corn
That steamers bring to the quay,
Bargains that much like love
Show an advantage to each
Party while favouring none,
Only the bargain itself
Following Nature's decree,
Blind to all other ideals,
Human, social, divine.

So it appeared to him,
Less than experienced, yet
Fearful of all the truths
Only experience can bring,
Jealous of it in others,
Women especially, when
Brought in a moment to bear

Casually, lightly on
Whatever matter at hand
Might thereby be resolved.
Not by him, alas.
That was the point, he knew,
Yielding up to her will
Choices that he should make,
Yielding in great things as small,
Held to her will, her eyes
Glancing around the room,
Popular as she is, heads
Turning as she goes by,
Making it perfectly clear
How, from the start, her life
Had not been held to a choice,
How in the future her course
Would not derive from that past.

There isn't a thing he can do,
Nothing to stem the slow
Chill that creeps in the night
Up from the toes to the neck,
Nothing to curtain his eyes
Closed though they were to the dark,
Staring at all the distinct
Unreliable fears
Peopling the walls of his head.

Now the bells, the fool bells
Fill it again with their grave
Sound of a musical march,
Marching in step in the Markt,
Marching upon the boards
Over the heads of a crowd
Gawping at something they'd seen
Time after time before,
Gawping as though it were new,

Something to write home about.
Bell after bell displayed
Not with a wooden handle,
Nothing so well-designed,
Only a cow-bell held
Fistfully by its strap,
Banged on the thigh and the knee
By men with solemn looks
Making their beastly sound.

Folk-art, he had to conclude
Sadly, since folk must have art,
Folk-art worthy of Swiss
Orderliness: severe,
Rational, thoroughly done,
Local, ingenious – like
The tourist hotel, indeed
Like the Hotel Bellevue.
Closing his eyes, he tried
Placing the sounds in some
Abstract innocuous context,
Meadows, a pretty box,
Something less human and grim:
Still the vision distracted,
Green leather trousers rubbed brown,
Rubbed by the bouncing bells,
Pairs of ridiculous bells
(Pairs of ridiculous shorts)
Green but with streaks of brown
Like a damp ski-slope in spring.

So much the better with eyes
Closed, and so much best with
Senses in general closed
To his problem, shutting up shop,
Testing the faithfulness,
Single-minded and pure,

That they with waywardness
Eagerly undermine.
Cruelty of desire
Casting soul-pledges aside,
Weakness of body turned
Back from the path it proposed.
Cadences falling, slow
Winding down of thoughts
Till in their stillness they
Told their tale of the sad
Hopelessness, passion and grief
Brought by men to their loves.

What was there left to do?
Where could he go? To leave
Cowardly, yes, and to stay
Foolish, but he was a fool,
Felt like a fool, a great
Grinning fool of a man
Twisting his hat in his hand,
Talking of Senancour,
Tracing on summits of schlag
Fork-tracks of mountaineers,
Laughing, and raising a glass
Over the tablecloth:
'Drink to the Roman Republic!'
Knowing that destiny frowns
Fiercely on great things as small,
Insignificant hopes,
Futile desires of men
Trapped in their theories of good.
Next year, then, will it be?
Shall we make reservations?
Are we mere tourists in our
Own as yet unexplained lives?
Shall our paths sweetly meet
Just as we once hoped they would?

Unseen the hidden Aare
Leaving the lake undisturbed,
Flowing on, who knows where,
And the lake so beautiful,
Just as it always was, there.

4

THE RIVALS

THE RIVALS

1 *Sachs*

Midsummer-day, the year's arch, is my name day.
Forever in the fullness of the year
Midsummer- and St John's day are the same day:
Johannestag, Johannes, Hans . . . . My dear,
Do you remember picking chanterelles
Whose creamy buttons showed above the moss
Like liquid notes that float from the clear bells
Of oboes on a misty day across
A meadow? We were in the little wood
That's scattered down the stream, a place so haunted
It charmed us from ourselves so that we could
Discover who we were, so that you wanted
To rest there for a while, your shoulder on
My shoulder . . . . And I am Hans, and not yet gone.

They grow where leaf-enhancing sunlight dapples
The mossy bank beside the talking stream,
Like apricots just stretching to be chapels
Or crumbling capitals of stone that dream
Of missing architraves. Loosed to your fingers
And light as pleated paper, into the basket
They twirl like trumpets. When the gatherer lingers
It is to seek a question, and then ask it:
What is the final form of our endeavours?
Is it to founder farthest from our faults?
To breast the wave that breaks, the arch that severs?
Or simply to set out, like these peach vaults
That leap up from the undemanding green
And do not care if they are never seen?

Across the emptiness that I am used to,
Something appears that's pointing to a place

That with a helping hand I'd be induced to
Leap to if I tried. It is your face,
Which asks in teasing silence if there is
Some simple reason why I live alone.
My eyes and tongue are mortal enemies.
Seeing and speaking are at odds. I own
A fatal gift for knowing how to wait,
For making the decisive move not cheerfully
Too soon, but overseriously, late;
Not with a reassuring smile, but tearfully,
As though I could not stretch across that void
Without one side or other being destroyed.

And after all, I would not wish to share
The empty life that sharing is designed
To fill. How could I come to you and stare
Into those willing eyes only to find
The blank reflection of my own disgust
At having nothing more to offer you?
And you? How long could you preserve your trust
In things that could not possibly be true,
Such as a purpose in the self-contained,
Feeling in the complacent, change in the old,
Or any wish to be unlike a pained
Observer of the tide of life, a cold
Unpenetrated heart of loneliness
Who's long moved on from his last known address?

That wild unsettled look is sprawled across
The squares of every life. Passing, you see
The zones of misery, the Martyr's Cross,
The selfish corners where a memory
Touches its grimy forelock for a drink,
The benches where the stiff mistakes nod on
Throughout an autumn's fury. Do you think
That love could ever change them? Would they be gone

After one season of your sweet patrol?
Sometimes I think they might. The clouds are blown
Across the moon in veils. The quietened soul
Sits of an evening on a still-warm stone
Within the hearing of a stream, while far
Above shines one bright unexpected star.

2 Beckmesser

My wicked comfort is that everyone
Knows what it's like: the ground pulled out from under
And all you thought you had achieved undone,
Reduced to stammering, a holiday wonder.
We each have this unique tremendous chance,
Luck carelessly worn, the gift of song,
The formula for love learned at a glance:
And then you realise you got it wrong.
But it is yours. Still is. You live with it,
This vast mistake committed without coercion.
The air is shaking with your lack of wit
And love's in shambles in your broken version.
Your whole life led to this derisive laughter.
This is where you stop. There's nothing after.

I don't trust them an inch. I know their ways.
Their sins define a civic history
That no remorse is able to erase,
And all are in my book. They have to be,
For I am Sixtus Beckmesser. I am
Town Clerk of Nuremberg. I write down all
That happens here. The bee, the oak, the lamb
Offer their services. In the Town Hall
Are deeds and registers, row upon row,
Room after room. The spider on the shelf
Knows everything a spider needs to know.

I am the Recording Angel. I am myself.
Nothing that's happened need have, nor will last
Unless I say so. I control the past.

It all comes to a preparation for
This moment. It gathers with proprietary
Fondness like a father at the door,
Hiding, to hear the ending of a story
That once when he was young he thought he knew.
It is the forbidden second chance of time.
It is the chalk scrawl of equations, true
At the proof. It is the undiscovered crime
That lies behind the questions of the present,
A history of expectation and
The characters of pleasant and unpleasant
Pieces in a game as yet unplanned
But somehow played already. It's a mad
Look at the future you've already had.

And then, the worst of failure is the thought
That no one else considers it a sin
Simply to be yourself. It's you who's caught
By this killed promise of the might-have-been,
You who had secretly expected better
And you who even now, as mental editor
Of these events, reverse their upshot, debtor
And bankrupt turned to cheated creditor.
How-Could-I is the seed of It's-Not-True,
Ruined-For-Ever of Let's-Call-A-Halt.
You learn to claim that all the time you knew
It wasn't yours but circumstance's fault,
A chance that led you into wanting what
You scarcely hoped for, and then added: 'Not'.

Why did I think the song itself would win
And so make true the only thing which feeds it?
The unfulfilled desire where we begin

Is where we end: imagination needs it.
It is the only good for which we long,
It is the consolation of our age,
It is the master passion of our song,
The private reason for the public rage.
Better to steal, if stealing there must be,
To show your hunger all that it has lost.
Better learn feelings from the melody,
Considering the dignity it cost.
Passions run on and leave you far behind:
Each one of them is not the least you mind.

3 *Sachs*

Why did I think that love itself would win
And so create the only thing it makes?
Song is the beauty we are perfect in.
Song is the interest our self-loathing takes.
How can we claim desire at second-hand
Or offer prizes to unhappiness,
Lonely as ever when we take our stand
And closing palms mock with their loud address?
Better to give, if giving there must be,
The things that can be shared only in art
And soothe the feelings with new melody:
Better the rules are broken than the heart.
Songs will redeem our passions if we let them.
Songs are the means by which we can forget them.

And then the future: scanning the empty track,
Faint cries upon the dusky air, the tall
Competitors look forward. And look back.
You find yourself in motion after all.
Whose is that presence breathing at your side?
Whose is the daunting shape whose step you share?
The body's largest organ seems to stride

Like thunder over mountains, everywhere.
You sense that for a lifetime you must wait
For life to give the signal it's begun.
In what you always hope is the last straight
You give your all, and think the race is won:
Acknowledge that your true role was to pace
Your own performance, which will not take place.

The song is his, and somehow he conceived it
Out of an air electric with his urge
To be, and bring to being. He received it
As birthright, testimony, pledge. A surge
Of human recognition left him sick
Of incompleteness, sick of the consequence
And drift of all the studious rhetoric
That forms the life of dullness and expense.
And so the song required its object, not
To gratify, but to absolve, to bless.
Without that answering instruction, what
Could a garden be but a rich wilderness,
Nature's last joke, with nothing left to choose
Between a worldly mistress and the muse?

Happy enough to know that you are there:
Your love is like a pillar, a reprieve.
It is enough to last me. What we share
Sustains a future over which I grieve,
Knowing our sharing has a natural end:
Your life outstretching mine simply in years
Defines a dizzy breach too deep to mend,
Both wound and weapon, fantasy and fears.
I see it waiting for you, undefined
Except as waiting. Like some wayward sprite
Looking to occupy a vacant mind
With haunting of a sort. And so it might,
Once it's invited there to take its chance
In the charmed wastefulness of ignorance.

The moon still hangs upon the morning hill
As if it had been blanched into a skull
Through night's dead influence. I see it still,
That mossy bone, that socket, that pale hull
Beached in the daylight on the travelling sky,
The doomed adventurer of all our dreams,
The false associate whose credible lie
Haunts our imaginings with borrowed beams.
No, it is not the sun. But very soon
I know I'll feel that massive warmth behind me.
Westward I'm gazing still, to keep the moon
Within my sight, but soon the sun will find me.
And it will shine, as yesterday it shone
Unstintingly. The moon will soon be gone.

5

Brahms in Thun

BRAHMS IN THUN

Who is that singular man upon the path
Winding from Hofstetten, his long black coat
Greying with age, the shawl over his shoulders
Fastened with a pin? The flannel shirt
Collarless, and the shabby leather satchel
Surely full of bohemian mysteries?

The urchins know who he is. He shoos them away
With the hat that's always in his pudgy hand.
The girls know who he is. When he draws near,
A trifle corpulent, full-bearded, grey,
They notice with a flutter of the heart
The piercing blue eyes of a younger man.

Who certainly notices them. He gives a bow,
A brief acknowledgement of what their eyes
Have searched for in his eyes. Then looks away.
This is not the time, nor ever will be,
For words to rob the unspoken melody
Of its elusive and absorbing fragrance.

It haunts him now. Its cadences arrive
Like the brief mysteries of flowers in spring,
Frail for the buttonhole, their scent soon gone.
But now in the dust of summer let him stand
And let the petals open, let them fall
In all their fullness to the reaching hand.

This morning, stepping from the deep-eaved villa
Rented from Herr Spring, half in its shadow,
He paused just for a moment, lit a cigar
And breathed at once the air and its aroma.
This is the mood of amiable resolution,
The piano as portico to an adventure.

He feels that he might stroke the Wellingtonia,
Whose roots beneath the hill drink in the lake,
While here by the railings at megalosaurus's height
Its branches stir in their Jurassic calm;
Stroke its rough hide as if it gave off sound,
As if the pine were strung to its very tip.

Even now the smoke continues its
Vague dispersal through the shadowed tree,
Lofting minutest particles in the warm air
To the pine's pinnacle, where the needles cease.
Although now he has passed along the path,
The stride determined, tobacco in clouds about him.

The tiles of the Thunerhof below are severe
To the meditative eye, the circular divan
In the Bellevue salon equally distracting.
There the Knechtenhofers' assembled guests
Would eat the famous composer half-alive
To occupy the lateness of the morning.

'Milord Ponsonby would wish that he
Were here, as we ourselves are glad to be:
The great artist in sounds, the sheet of the lake
Covered with quavers of sails, a glass or two
To toast Vienna and to hear a tale
Of Elgin, ruins, and a grand concerto . . .'

A lion, then, among the jackals who
Would lift their jaws from working, prick their ears
At rumours of a richer feast elsewhere
And leave their crumbs of carrion behind
For the bored waiters of the Speiseterrasse.
Take heart: the Bains de Bellevue are not for him.

On, on, to the Schüssel in the Plätzli,
The beer ingratiating, dizzy and blond,

The company reliable, with shouting laughter,
The schnitzels overlapping their plates all round,
Heavy as dewlaps of long-slumbering hounds,
The flower fading on the creased lapel.

But in the mind, where flowers never fade,
There lives one favoured face that is a smile,
A smile that is a voice: '*O komme bald*!'
'Come soon, come soon! Before the May winds blow,
Before the thrush sings in the wood, oh come!
If you would see me once again, oh come!'

The voice is hers, and yet the song is his.
Who can be certain where the yearning lies?
Her lips are parted, and his notes come out.
Her throat swells with the thrilling melody
That will make others weep; so she and he
Survive their shout of grief, inviolable.

But is it grief? Not joy, perhaps? She gave
Him joy. He gave it back as if it were
Some sort of tender, self-inflicted wound:
'Often in my dreams I hear you calling,
Calling outside my door. But no one wakes,
Nobody is awake to let you in.'

What does he think they mean, these words?
Fate is in them, also resolution.
Death, too, is there, and also a wild hope:
'Come, then, for one last time, for you will find me
Gone from a world that has no place for us.
But if you come, oh if you come, come soon.'

And will one come again, will such a one?
His Fräulein Spies, the charming Rhinemaiden,
Herma, Herminche, Hermione-ohne-o?
He follows her to Wiesbaden, full-tilt

At his Third Symphony, sets Groth for her.
He's never in his life written so fast.

And he'll produce her for the Widmanns (guilty
Of curiosity about the work
She has inspired). Rigorous torture by song's
Their punishment: the jovial composer
And his Krefeld songstress will come to them with skewers
('*Spiessen und stangen!*') next Wednesday after dinner.

Wonderful Thun . . . . The steamer on the lake
Hoots at the afternoon; its paddles ply
The Aare to the harbour where he sees
Such parasols in clusters, greeting, retreating.
Beyond, a train is puffing into the station
Like an old gentleman expecting treats.

Later he might allow himself to walk
Down there again, a brandy at the Freienhof,
And in the Markt the smell of girls and herring.
And will one come again, will such a one?
It haunts him like something about to disappear.
He tries to put a name to it, but fails.

Perhaps it is something he has always missed,
The sound of laughter in another room,
Hands at his knee, hands tugging him away,
The playing, the watching, the kissing and the dancing,
The faces echoing their other faces,
That strange projection of the self, like art.

Some melodies are statements like the mountains,
The Stockhorn, Niesen, and the Blümlisalp,
Claiming their definition of the sky,
Others elusive as the mist which rises
Like half-remembered dreams from the still lake
In which the sky and mountains have been drowned.

And they exchange their notes in playful ways
That echo all these harmonies of nature
Where one thing, though itself, reveals another:
Fields broken by trees, forest by pasture,
The levels of the Aare linked by weirs,
Its course shaped both by broken land and water.

The little town itself, with its red roofs,
Rises like a flowering of the earth,
A human watchfulness that celebrates
The parting of the river from the lake
In boyish determination, that sees its future
Clear, and makes its watery business there.

And the Schloss, its profile out of fairy-tales,
Throws up its pointed turrets at the sky,
Casements of trance, imprisonment or longing
Where distance is for once the only meaning,
Its central slab of tiles uncannily
Matching the Stockhorn like a falling cadence.

And will one come again, will such a one?
And what on earth would happen if she did?
Herma, Herminche, Hermione-ohne-o,
The voice embodying the melody,
The melody abstracting from the heart,
The heart enchanted by an opening mouth.

'I am a man who's getting to those years
Where he quite easily does something stupid,
And so I have to doubly watch myself.'
And Clara thinks she's being left in the cold,
Dear Clara, arbiter, his earliest muse,
Old lady at the keyboard in a cap.

Who, when her darling Robert in his slippers
Left her and ran out through the carnival

To throw his person into the Rhine and madness,
Preserved herself for music and her children,
Year upon year preparing for her concerts
Like a devoted priestess at the altar.

Who taught him out of tragedy to know
That feelings are firmly locked within the stave
Lest they uncover foulness: what would she say?
The fingers scramble like waves upon the shore,
Tides of regret advance to their conclusion,
Storming their beaches, where her profile bows.

There are mistakes too terrible to be made,
When to approach them, as to an upstairs room
Where light invites the idle passer-by,
Is to stand upon a brink of fascination
Whose logic is a desecration and
Whose music is a series of farewells.

All that this art in its bodily abstraction
Has seriously learned to do: to exult in pain
And be stoical in pleasure, to be triumphant
With propriety and reserved in ceremony,
To take grief into fury and out of it again,
He had for long with mastery acquired.

His mood now is a matter of resolution,
Where resolution has no certain hope
To pronounce an equal love impossible
In waves of thunder shot with trickles of light,
To embrace the damage of the soul with joy
And to erect the architecture of tenderness.

His hand moves over the page like a flock of birds
Seeking rest in snow, their tracks a relic
Of the enduring passage of a hunger
Across an infinite waste, a fragile heartbeat,

The Stockhorn, Niesen, and the Blümlisalp,
At once forbidding and familiar.

Quick, catch their flight . . . The hand continues to move,
The quavers swarm, the sheets fall from the piano,
The rhythms fight it out, the prey's in sight,
Crisp noble chords, the strings making decisions
That their invisible fingers lead them to,
The next idea that lies in wait for them.

The only respite is a dark Kaffee.
The ritual itself is stimulating:
His brass pot from Vienna with its spigot;
Its porcelain stand; the little burner moving
Its blue flame like a crocus underneath;
The grinding of the Mokka from Marseilles.

And a cigar, of course. And in its wreaths,
The music for a moment laid to rest,
He lives within the mood it has created:
And will one come again, will such a one?
And what on earth would happen if she did?
How to accommodate that bodied voice?

Herma, Herminche, Hermione-ohne-o!
Is it too late? Isn't the paradox
Just this: the one mistake committed is
The one that will transcend both fear and error
And in its act be no mistake at all?
And will one come again, will such a one?

Somewhere in his mind the names proceed
Like cases that have come to shape a law:
Clara, of course, Agathe, Julie, Lisl,
And all the singers of his Frauenchör
Whose voice and beauty caught his ear and eye,
Music's muses, music's priestesses.

They ring him round with their accusing looks.
He kneels before them in contrition, asking
Of song if the perfection of its moods
And of its utterance has power to
Redeem the soul of a defective man.
And song, as usual, has no sort of answer.

Nor does Kaffee. And nor do Frau Widmann's buttery
Plum pastries. Nor does the Wellingtonia.
Nor does that broad and energising vista
Across the lake where paddle-steamers ply,
The Stockhorn, Niesen, and the Blümlisalp,
Each reassuring as a reputation.

For there it is. The music must be written.
And Fräulein Spies will have her début in
Vienna. And Karlsgasse num. 4 is only
An old bear's den, almost a hermit's cell.
And the Bernese summer, like every summer since
The beginning of the world, will soon be over.

And with the summer over, who can say
What may be found in the satchel of mysteries?
Wonderful Thun . . . . The watchful fairy Schloss,
The midwife of his own late blossoming,
Herma, Herminche, Hermione-ohne-o,
The Trio, the Sonatas, and the Songs.

'Come, then, for one last time, for you will find me
Gone from a world that has no place for us.
But if you come, oh if you come, come soon!'
The instruments inscribe their own enticements
Upon the holy movement of a heart
Too long alone to know when it is teasing.

'It comes to me, this thing, whatever it is,
Like the spring flowers that steal upon the senses

And drift like scent away. Then comes the word
That holds it before my eye until it pales
Like the grey mist, and like a scent it dies.
Yet still a tear calls fragrance from its bud.'

That tear is music, emotion's memory,
And God forbid there should be story in it.
The good Herr Doktor with the forget-me-not eyes
Strides on, the emperor of a world of sound
So pure he scarcely sees that its grand truth
Is fatally wedded to the human voice.

6

THE FIFTH MARQUESS

THE FIFTH MARQUESS

Sailing from Menton with his Chinese dogs,
He thought about the scale of things, his dream
Of voyaging, its obvious analogues:
An innocent and condescending stream
Joining the swarming heave of the old ocean,
Life seeking life, stillness absorbing motion.

Impossible to stage in Anglesey
The terraces and repartee of France,
Impossible to fill diurnity
With the expressive gestures of the dance,
But something old and cold here satisfied
His Grace's arch inconsolable pride.

The dogs are sleepy from their morning milk.
The scent of sofas maddens them. They crowd
The thickets of table-legs and rustling silk,
Sniffing the urns and whimpering aloud
For something of the landscape they were bred from,
Seeking the kindly hand that they were fed from.

But he is tired of them already, toys
Of a passing season, part of a disguise
Requiring their squashed faces not their noise.
He could not bear the liquid slavish eyes
That looked up from his crooked embroidered arm
As though no other place could be as warm.

Disguises! Another setting for his face,
That unique jewel! No expense is spared
To give its sparkling an appropriate space.
Lives are borrowed and experience shared.
All of them, he is so thoroughly through with them,
He doesn't know, has never known what to do with them.

His Grace as Gracchus, haunting drawing-rooms,
His Grace as Venus, ogling for the apple,
His Grace designing the ancestral tombs,
Building a theatre in the family chapel
Where he will condescend to spend much time,
A Japanese auguste in pantomime.

There was a fourth, but can there be a sixth?
Impossible to think of the occasion.
'Sticks and stones may hurt, and stones and sticks.'
Life takes its course, and so does reputation.
One day, he thought, he would return to France.
One day he'd find the stillness of the dance.

But now, descending to the Straits, he saw
Clearly for once how he must play his part,
A heron among herons by the shore,
Lovely, although unloved, clutching his heart
By waters flushed with a peculiar tide,
Not sea, not river, always unsatisfied.

7

WALLACE STEVENS AT THE CLAVIER

WALLACE STEVENS AT THE CLAVIER

I

I am the amateur of tragedy,
The Knave of Hearts, the Quince of Ives,
My fingers laddering the ivories,
Idly chromatic, quintessence of white and black,
White of the inner thigh, the black of lace
And all that jazz, the hootchie-cootchie-coo.
Why play the Concord Sonata if you could
Play Chopin, or both, or Chopsticks for that matter?
For music is apprentice to desire,
To yearning, or the comedy of kisses,
Here at this keyboard, thinking of wanting you.

II

But music has no pages. It expands
To fill the empty spaces where it plays
Like any calculated melancholy.
And memory agrees with Meredith
That we inhabit all that we have done,
Inhabit the idea of it, which is
The parent fountain of our deepest life,
Opposed to that of perishable blood.
Then let, out of the fury of our fingers,
Something like a melody be heard
Beneath the stabbing of a tenor thumb.

III

Too late, exclaims the Spoiler of Satisfactions!
But even at this moment there's a hope,
Like the false gleams of sunset that distil
Easy beneficence across a lake,
That all defeat may be postponed, that night
Might just reserve its absolutes for once.
Pages of Brahms that say so come to hand
With all their loving dedications and
With all their folded blackened corners, locus
Of an ecstatic passion hymned as it departs
In half-acceptance of imagined loss.

IV

The piano steers into the summer falls,
Floating through cresses and blue butterflies,
The music of an idle voyaging,
Portrait of a girl in a chapeau
That might have graced the lake at Fontainebleau.
I push the pole and steady in the stream
Of melody, its tink-a-tink-a-tink,
Canoe canoodlings, all those forgotten things.
My foot treads on the Bechstein's creaking step
As if to hold the evening from its fall.
The page is ending with a double bar.

V

You might reflect, as fellows often do,
On inch-thick cold roast beef and English mustard,
A bold adventure for an afternoon!
Viburnum springs back from the fingers but
Its scent remains. In navy, white and grey,

The geese compose a print in Japanese
With questioning necks attendant in splayed feathers.
And should the sun be parsimonious,
Reminding us of summers lost, no matter.
Since summers once existed, let us go
Over to the Canoe Club to make hay.

VI

I turn to Opus 118, A Major,
Andante teneramente, opening with
Three wistful notes like fingers reaching out
That find no other fingers but describe
An airy gesture of their own, which says:
I have no otherwhere to turn but here,
C sharp, B and D, interrogation,
Reflection, memory, hope and regret.
These are my mood's containment. They expand.
They stretch. And fall back into rumination.
Too late? Too late! Yet, not perhaps too late.

VII

C sharp, B and D; then C sharp, B
And A: a lifting of the little phrase
That signifies some sort of faint resolve
Embodied in the awkward reach of fingers.
Now this is truly Elsie, truly you
As once you self-expectantly became,
Waiting in Reading for my New York letters,
An intermezzo in a greater opus
Peculiar to that suspended state,
Pellucid opuscule to make us blink,
A glimpse into the rawness of the heart.

VIII

Now I can read my poems as I read
This music, as a pure recall of feeling,
Finding in their notes some thoughts of you,
A kind of thinking of thinking of wanting you,
Not as you are, but as you were composed
By that impulsive hand that is first love
Tracing in fitful touch the sound of shape,
The shape of beauty that is in the mind.
The memory that falters in the fingers,
The fingers that press down upon the keys
Like the great roots of trees, slaking a thirst.

IX

The piano is a threshold that will bring
Beauty to its imperishable heaven.
Here is an eye the straying fingers say,
And *one by one, the lashes of that eye*
In cadences like modesty, or flashing fire,
Until the whole assembly in the mind
Is she herself, the true Badroulbadour!
If once it was mortality I feared,
As I imagined her a prey to worms,
Now it is time's indifference, the slow
Ceasing of an enchantment, and long silence.

X

The comeliest girl in Reading, Pennsylvania,
Entirely blonde and pale, a childlike skin,
Wearing the biggest hat you ever saw:
Who would not weep to fail to win her hand?
I have seen lesser marvels that were wronged:

68

The one false note that habit likes to play,
Rugs soiled, wild lemons left to rot.
If life were perfect, then we might declare
That there is nothing in the scale of things
To cause such grief, as this bleak aftermath:
To treat a wife as if she were mere ash.

XI

The worms consume only the accidence
And must themselves be numbered for her name
As though it were the answer to a riddle,
The single thought of her, *out of the tomb:*
Badroulbadour, we bring Badroulbadour.
But ah, the substance: that is poetry,
That pours reality into the mind
Like an extraordinary cabernet,
A cabinet confined of cabernet
Left for the dozen years it needs to be,
Left for a married lifetime, if needs be.

XII

Aladdin hidden in the hammam knew
The singing of the blood inside his head
That shamed the elders to accuse Susannah,
But his Badroulbadour was truly blameless
And bore her body ceremoniously
Among her maidens to the secret bath,
A little moon outshining a host of stars,
A moon unveiled as unimagined sunlight,
The spells upon her cheek with a burnt rose
Teaching him conjurations of desire
And shattering for ever his repose.

XIII

Who could have thought such beauty as he saw?
A veil was lifted from his eyes and he
Was good for nothing and he knew no rest.
His head was music and the music silk.
And everything was changed inside his head
By what he had not known to be outside it.
This was the world of all the possible worlds,
Standing in its uniqueness, shadowless.
This was the earth he loved enough to die.
His mother wept for the stone of her heart's fruit
And for her boy's ambition, and its object.

XIV

What, if we are gifted, is that gift
But consciousness that we might give again?
As the young poet, dreaming in violet cities,
Gives back to villages their consciousness
Of wonder and invisible esteems.
As the poor lover, pacing the lonely streets,
Bids the Ifrit of his imagination
Describe for him a palace of desire
In which his love might live, as he has lived,
In the abstractions of a fictive night
That turns all light to fathomable sound.

XV

Aladdin was a tailor's son and knew
How to sit cross-legged in humility,
A shearsman of sorts, plying a simple craft
That clothed the world with his imagination,
Graced in good fortune to become a god,

As poets are who conjure palaces
And other worlds for beauty to inhabit.
The birds that flocked about its turrets cried
Humiliating cries of their raw needs
And melons rotted in untended gardens
And the world declined as the blue music played.

XVI

The bridegroom's music is a spectral waltz
That severed fingers play in shuttered rooms
After another day has done its stuff.
I have torn off too many calendars
To claim a quiddity in certain bones
That let a person jig, or not, at will.
We are automata who turn and turn
Until we stop and pray ourselves to peace.
And yet I lie, waiting until the day.
Apart from me, shut in the robber dark
The music suffocates beneath its lid.

XVII

Throughout the night I tried to dream that you
Were once again beside me, and you were.
You lay in perfect weight and quiet breathing,
Famous and private, my familiar.
And yet throughout the night I was alone,
It being, after all, only a dream.
The lamp that won you, that you gave away,
The lamp, the lamp is truly lost, the palace
Disappeared that housed Badroulbadour.
If somewhere it exists it is not here.
If somewhere you exist I am not there.

XVIII

We live together in the house, apart,
One side the womenfolk's, the other mine.
Walls are no hindrance in a garden where
You'll find a variety of lilies and
A giant white rabbit that is eating them.
A heavy man is strolling beneath his thoughts
And thirty-cent cigar smoke out of Tampa,
Reflecting on the freedoms of the place,
The conversations in the evening air,
The memories of decisive secateurs
Or Holly nude in the magnolia tree.

XIX

Of roses on the piano, by her hand
Cut and displayed, is little to be said.
They are the young god fallen into sleep,
The lacrimae of some outworn amour
That throws a truculent scent into the air,
The faded cousins of an adjutant brandy
Placed to excuse the pianist's rapt mistakes.
They are the moving mezzotints of nature,
Against which sound proclaims eternity
In its grave absolution from a pain
That rises from the keys into those roses.

XX

When Adolph Weinman came to look at you,
You were not thirty. Immortality
Was in his gift, like the assassin's knife.
His Liberty beside the rising sun
With sheaves, his aviatrix Mercury,

Close-helmeted, erect, scanning horizons:
These were the coin of the new century,
The ikons of a need that strode the world.
O woman with the hair of a pythoness,
You are the profile of a currency
Placed in the palms of beggars like a blessing!

XXI

Your nose is spared from sharpness by the touch
Of many ignorant fingers, and your cheek
Faded to an unnatural smoothness, ghostly
Upon the familiar features of your face.
You flit like Mercury from soul to soul.
When once I spread my gems of marvel out
Like fruit upon a dish, and saw you take
Your fancy there, as you might twirl a fan,
You lead me to the understated darkness
Of this dead room, where on a dresser of deal
I heap my loose change like cold memories.

XXII

Dish after dish, the fluted pie-crust lifts,
Revealing baked asparagus in cream,
Coffined crusaders, holy in repose,
Dreaming their dream, in green and purple greaves,
Of a stout thrusting at the pagan shrine.
Who would have stomach for such courtesies
As their devout adventuring requires?
I have grown large on cake and other fancies
And the slow pace that goes with their collection,
The paper sack clutched in a singular hand,
The sidewalk shadowed with autumnal hues.

XXIII

To cast aspersions on asparagus
Becomes the mental amorist's lament.
And other table manners: offering
The tilted pinot to an untouched glass
Or violence to an alligator pear,
Tossing a napkin like a sheet aside,
Leaving the table as he leaves a bed
With little done and everything unsaid.
I tried to give up poetry for you.
Sensing you thought that it divided us,
Carved love-seat not quite wide enough for two.

XXIV

The lake I painted bled into the earth.
Its cradle had been spat on by the Witch
And a foul umber stained its ultramarine.
No matter, since I was that vista's hero,
My easel packed, whistling at distances
Beyond the comfortable close-cropped sward.
For what beside my brogues was waveletted
Grew pale at length to an inviting surface.
Which I declined, however, with good grace,
Since lakes are rings, a marriage not a voyage.
You only come upon another shore.

XXV

Your eyes stared at my waistcoat as we danced
Like the beaked nightbird in a jewelled wood.
It was the dance of lawyers, dance of bears,
The ceremonious duty of a feast.
My leather bindings, my Impressionists,

My palace: all in hostage to the dance,
The dance itself in hostage to your beauty.
And yet your beauty faded, and in turn
You gave the wicked Darwish what he asked for,
Thinking it of little value, as he claimed,
New lamps for old, and changed my life for ever.

XXVI

Holly at the piano, gradus ad
Parnassum, Holly with a checking account,
Child of that grandeur off Tehauntepec
Which once returned us to our primal dreams.
Yet folly is to remind us of corruption,
The futile colours of old ecstasies.
Vassals of Vassar, serving out your term
As any whipped novitiate will do,
Remember the prayers to your earthly fathers
And darn your stockings well! The moon will rise
Upon those blues, those pinks, and coffee creams.

XXVII

When gods grow old they settle by their fires
As outcasts do, their buckets glowing with coals,
And starry music turns to honky-tonk.
Through all our separation music has made
Its distillation of the residues,
Urged to its abstractions from my fear
Of losing them, yet still they swarm at will.
They weigh my fingers in a rising tangle
That now hangs like a haunting over me,
A scattering, a drenching, inescapable
As winds of history across the sidewalks.

XXVIII

Would you arrive attendant at that door,
Sleep-wearied, in a fantasy of sounds
That bring you walking into wakefulness?
The chords are puzzles in your uncombed head.
Their intervals narrow your half-closed eyes
To fathom them, for they are bodiless.
You have some memory of being wooed
By such a sound, in such a darkened place,
Where a familiar tramp drips with desire
For shelter, seeing you raise an anxious hand
And turn behind the storm-screen to your dreams.

XXIX

They think you are the wicked Witch from Oz
And I a beast in thrall, in human shape.
Or else you are quite mad, and put away,
And I your keeper. I chase them from the gate
Like little rosy daisies, with a stick.
And always there is your piano, and its bones.
We sleep in distant wings of the flying house,
Heavy with longing for the ordinary.
You are an apparition of my mind,
Locked in the palace of my wilfulness,
Invisible within my poetry.

XXX

The emperor of tawdry treats is still
The emperor of some distinct idea
Which in the being conceived is quite transformed,
As ice and salt are turned, to defy death,
And nothing could be more magnificent.

So I have heard that men at their final breath
Look round them at the strange relations there
And wish for such a coldness on their tongue
That grief might find appropriate celebration
In beggar's food. And yet an emperor
May go a progress through a beggar's guts.

XXXI

An ounce of Cretan bhang is strong enough
To kill an elephant: the Darwish dies!
And yet, of course, the Darwish does not die.
He is the evil one, the Moor, in league
With the eternal Separator of Friends.
Knowing this, we know he'll reappear.
Once in state I held the throne of China
Where crimson eaves were battered by the rain
And the leaves flew wildly. All that I have left
Is that dark place where beauty is recreated,
Brought by the worms into the gate of heaven.

XXXII

Said Hamlet of Polonius to the King:
He is at supper. Not where he eats, but where
He's eaten. This is a prince's poetry.
So much for the company of worms.
And so his play, like any music, plays
Upon the octaves of the living spine
And the hair rises erect, as at a spook
That sways her intermezzo from the grave
To speak mad words or clutch your frozen fingers.
The worm's your only emperor for diet
But poetry's the only heaven we have.

8

Thun 1947

THUN 1947

My mother's evenings: Brahms in Hungarian mood,
Her nails clicking, cigarette ash bombing the keys,
Or feeding the folded hem of a holiday frock
Beneath the pile-driving needle of her Singer
Like a blind woman feeling along a shelf;
Rapt, and to me mysterious, movement of fingers
When notes and stitches stuck and ravelled in lurches
And the face became a mask of intent, like a mirror.

The frock was packed, with its promise of release
From necessary details of dailiness
Like a page from a history of her future life
Torn out to be secretly looked at and admired,
And my father pressed the locks of the fibre suitcase,
Keeping the key safe, with its buff card tag,
And took us off to Europe, on a whim,
As if to inspect it, like a plate, for damage.

The train rattled across recovered France,
Exploring in its ruined library
Cities like classics of a forgotten age.
And my father, younger than my daughters now,
Weary with war and with austerity,
Resolved upon adventure, secure in knowing
The unassailable status of families,
Sacred in all their peculiarities.

His hand rose to his moustache, that moment
Of amusement, self-appraisal, ruminative
Pleasure that would precede a little laugh,
Forefinger smoothing down its surface, the thumb
Concealed, but stroking its base away from the lips,
A flourish that seemed to say: 'Well, here we are!'

Yes, the operation was successful.
Time had smiled on his contrivances.

The suitcase closed in London was opened in
The Bernese Oberland, and if it carried
Its ghostly baggage of separated lives
Across the shores of partings, beyond the past
With its leading questions and tacit promises,
It was not now to say. Our trinity
Was an old romance of sorts, somewhat on show,
Somewhat delayed, yet proving all its worth.

Suddenly I was running across the gravel paths
That were hot to the foot and blinding until dusk.
A close heat settled on the hotel gardens
Where butterflies collapsed upon the borders
And the heavy bee, dragging its dusty pelt,
Grappling and steadying its petal like
A squat wrestler, knew the single thing
That gave its furious purpose to the summer.

Dishes were brought to white tablecloths
By smiling waiters: Kässuppe and dark bread,
Ovals of veal, medallions in their jus,
Yellow and red pears, small Kaffees,
And after dinner the band beneath the trees
Played clumsier and bearlike versions of
The miniature marches and the model polkas
Pricked out by needles in their fretted cases.

Here were my first fireworks, bought to be saved
For days in their coloured paper and thin fuses,
Secretly guarded in quiet wonder for being,
Like books, the labels of all the strange events
That they contained, continually touched,
Till their small narratives burned on the hotel gravel

On the First of August, the Swiss National Day,
Lighting the darkness and the underside of leaves.

And other pleasures: the twenty-centime pieces
Dealt out as in a game and frequently
Replenished, like but unlike sixpences,
Disks of garlands sliding into machines
With an antebellum freedom, a welcoming chlunk
That delivered their boxed portions of *Kaugummi*
With the clatter and swagger of the everyday,
As though this magical life had never stopped.

I was ten, leggy and long before the age
When we are locked into our sex like a punishment.
Every day I walked along the quay
From the Freienhof to the wooden Flussbad's faded
Chocolatey violet, its louvred cubicle half-doors
Clicking and swinging like saloons in westerns,
With the pouches of costumes wrung out and hanging
On rails, smelling of twisted wool and oil.

There I would leap and be swept away in daring
Along the rapid Aare tasting of snow,
A shouting head carried along in the current
And what I shouted lost in the voice-filled air,
Till the soles of my feet settled on sodden wood,
The barrier spanning the width of the rushing river
To keep its bathers from spilling and flowing for ever,
And I was laughing and buoyant, and I could swim.

For the sadness of the seasons and their songs
My star-limbed childhood had no ready ear,
Yet somewhere on the air were all the sounds
That all Thun's summers ever made or heard,
The song itself of song's entitlement
To name the nameless feelings of the heart,

Groth's 'Wie Melodien . . .' which, set by Brahms,
Became his theme for evanescent love:

> 'Like melodies, there is this thing
> That haunts but will not stay,
> Like flowers that come in Spring
> And drift like scent away.
>
> A spoken word begins
> To shape it for my eyes,
> When like a mist it thins
> And like a breath it dies.
>
> Yet still within each verse
> A tender fragrance sleeps,
> Coaxed from the bud's tight purse
> By an eye that almost weeps.'

It passed me by upon the summer air
As to a wren the purpose of the gods.
It drifted on, beyond the pleasure gardens,
Above the little steamer on the lake
Where couples on the benches at the stern
Half heard its poignant message and reached out
To hold each other as the shoreline passed
And evening settled on the villages.

Now the fireflies rose and fell, in motions
Contrary to any eye which watched them,
And lamps were lit upon the terraces.
The grown-ups talked, sometimes to themselves,
Sometimes to other guests, in dialogue
Whose antiphons, embellished by tobacco,
Evaporated into the still branches
Of lofty trees, gaunt guardians of the night.

There Numa, stumbling after the old lawyer
His master, could bear at last to take the air

84

Or sit at his laced boots, panting with a grin.
'*Il est malade, tu sais, ce drôle de chien*'
Said our friend. We never knew what the illness was,
Although it was insisted on at length,
So much so that the man himself was known
To us, bearded, pince-nez'd, as 'Malade Chien'.

And Malade Chien gave me when we left
A three-inch wooden bow-legged bulldog
Covered in tan napped cloth, with bright glass eyes
And a painted scowl. It wasn't an ornament.
It wasn't a toy. But a little of the spirit
Of that stocky optimistic doggy life
Which had escaped the rheumy tottering Numa
And his lonely master, seated side by side.

Whatever my father found to say to him
In the weighed deference of conceded language
And the smiles of its imperfect understanding
I never knew, but ran away and played
Upon the baking terraces, like water
That seeks its secret knowledge of gravity,
Spreading itself in a mindless bestowal of favour
Upon the earth which is its safe domain.

Chips of gravel like heavy lumps of sugar,
Feathers, the blood spots of geranium,
Dried larvae, husks: the casual waste of summer,
And a dog's nose reaching down to sniff my play.
Poor Numa, half a century dead and more,
His master, too. My parents twelve years gone,
Though moving briefly in these lines of mine,
Sitting together, piecing out their French.

All that survives of those long days is what
My parents built for me in reaching out
Towards each other, something like an arch,

A space of joy, above me, out of my sight
But in my interest, the inscrutable
Design of their shared, not solitary life
Which an unsearching boy must keep somewhere
Like a toy too old for him, that cost too much.

High on the tilted uplands above the lake,
Just for a moment, I became myself,
Not for the first and not the only time
But at the end of something, and a beginning,
There on a grazed meadow at Goldiwil,
Knowing the distance between the Alps and me
To be no more than a foot-throb from the earth
Beneath me, yet somehow further than the stars.

In some unvisitable yet certainly
Recorded locus of our continuum
I am there still, alive from top to toe:
The lock of hair falling above a grin,
Falling like the long end of my belt,
The cricket shirt, the elbows brown and crooked,
The deep shorts, and the socks reaching to the knees,
The sandals doubly buckled, slightly turned in.

And long I stare at myself without staring back,
For the past, though winding, is a one-way street
And the future unfolds few maps. To be alone
Is a condition of the observing brain,
And something that's remote is better seen,
Like stars or mountains. And the heart goes out
Fiercely if frailly from its uncertain darkness,
Like coloured fires along the terraces.

ACKNOWLEDGEMENTS AND NOTES

The Solitary Life

First published by the Clutag Press in a limited edition in 2005.

2.8: Seneca is quoted in Petrarch's *De Vita Solitaria*, Book 2.

9: The story of the fiddler, Basile, is from Mistral.

11.14: cf. *'ma 'l vento ne portava le parole'* (Petrarch, *Canzoniere*, 267).

15.5–8, 14: cf. *'. . . et eunt homines mirari alta montium, et ingentes fluctus maris, et latissimes lapsus fluminum et Oceani ambitum, et gyras siderum, et reliquunt se ipsos . . .'* (Augustine, *Confessions*, X.viii.15). For the ascent of Mont Ventoux, see Petrarch's letter of 26 April 1336 in *Familiarium rerum libri*, iv.

16: cf. *'Medusa e l'error mio m'àn fatto un sasso / d'umor vano stillante'* (Petrarch, *Canzoniere*, 366).

17.13–14: cf. *'L'aura che'l verde laura e l'aureo crine'* (Petrarch, *Canzoniere*, 246).

21, 22: St Augustine.

23.9–14: The point about Hannibal is made in Petrarch, *Secretum*, the third dialogue.

26.8: *'Tarda sit illa dies et nostro serior ævo'* (Ovid, *Metamorphoses*, xv.868).

26.14: *'Vivo son io e tu se' morto ancora'* (Petrarch, *Triumphus Mortis*).

27.3–4: Petrarch first saw Laura, and also heard of her death, on 6 April.

28.1–2: See note to 2.8 above.

30: See Nicholas Mann, *Petrarch*.

31: See J. H. Newman, *An Essay on the Development of Christian Doctrine*, 1845, p. 63.

Coleridge in Stowey

First published in the *Times Literary Supplement*, no. 5389, 14 July 2006.

The epigraph, written at some time between April and June 1803, can be found in Coleridge's *Notebooks* (no. 1394 in the first volume of Kathleen Coburn's edition). The poem purports to be a meditation in winter beginning beneath the lime tree of 'This Lime-Tree Bower my Prison'.

50: 'little dear Heart' is a phrase that Coleridge uses of his son Derwent (*Notebooks*, no. 1820).

Arnold in Thun

First published in *Essays in Criticism*, vol. LV, no. 3, July 2005.

Nothing is certainly known about Arnold's 'Marguerite'. Park Honan's marvellously ingenious theory that she came from an émigré French Huguenot family, summer neighbour to the Arnolds in the Lake District during his early adolescence, is not much helped by the impression that Arnold gives of only being able to see her in Switzerland and by the circumstances revealed by the Marguerite poems themselves. He wrote to Clough on 29 September 1848: 'Tomorrow I repass the Gemmi and get to Thun: linger one day at the Hotel Bellevue for the sake of the blue eyes of one of its inmates; and then proceed by slow stages . . . to . . . England' and on 23 September 1849: 'I am here in a curious and not altogether comfortable state: however tomorrow I carry my aching head to the mountains and to my cousin the Blumlis Alp . . . Yes, I come, but in three or four days I shall be back here, and then I must try how soon I can ferociously turn towards England.' Apart from the poems themselves, there is no other corroborating material. The metre of the poem is Arnold's invention for 'Rugby Chapel' and other poems.

The Rivals

First published in *Agenda*, vol. 42, no. 1, Spring 2006.
In Wagner's *Die Meistersinger von Nürnberg*, convention requires that since Eva is herself the prize for the song awarded at the town's Midsummer Festival, the young knight Walther von Stolzing who loves her, and whom she loves, should win it and her. His coaching in this by Hans Sachs is a self-sacrifice on the part of Sachs, who himself loves her. Sixtus Beckmesser, more resolute than Sachs in his pursuit of Eva, is seen here as in some ways his double, more obviously conservative in his art, but no less in need of human love.

Brahms in Thun

First published in *The Poetry Review*, vol. 95, no. 2, Autumn 2005.
The words of the penultimate stanza are a version of the poem by Klaus Groth that Brahms set as the first of his *Fünf Lieder* (opus 105) of 1885–6:

> *Wie Melodien zieht es*
> *Mir leise durch den Sinn*
> *Wie Frühlingsblumen blüht es*
> *Und schwebt wie Duft dahin.*

> *Doch kommt das Wort und fasst es*
> *Und führt es vor das Aug*
> *Wie Nebelgrau erblasst es*
> *Und schwindet wie ein Hauch.*

> *Und dennoch ruht im Reime*
> *Verbogen wohl ein Duft*
> *Den mild aus stillem Keime*
> *Ein feuchtes Auge ruft.*

I give another translation of the poem after stanza 12 of 'Thun 1947'. Brahms reused the tune of this song (though with a different rhythm) as the second theme of the first movement of the second Violin Sonata of 1886, written in Thun and evocative of his feelings for Hermine Spies. Spies eventually married a lawyer, and died in 1893, aged thirty-six. Clara and Robert are Clara and Robert Schumann.

The Fifth Marquess

First published in the *London Magazine*, April/May 2006.

Wallace Stevens at the Clavier

First published in *Areté*, issue 17, Autumn 2005.
Many of the details of this poem are drawn from Stevens's *Letters*, ed. Holly Stevens (1967), or from Peter Brazeau, *Parts of a World: Wallace Stevens Remembered* (1983). Among the works of Stevens evoked in the poem are 'The Worms at Heaven's Gate', 'Le Monocle de Mon Oncle' (whose form the poem adopts), 'Peter Quince at the Clavier', 'The Emperor of Ice Cream' and 'The Man with the Blue Guitar'.

Thun 1947

First published in the *Times Literary Supplement*, no. 5379, 5 May 2006.
The original of Groth's poem is given in the note to 'Brahms in Thun' above.